# Get
# Acquainted
# With

# Jesus

## Barbara Bruce and Larry Beman

# INTRODUCTION

"The Risen Christ by the Sea" (To order a full-color print of this art, contact The Fellowship of Merry Christians, P.O. Box 895, Portage, Michigan 49081-0895.)

## Does the Following Describe You?

Do you ever feel as if your life is out of control?

Do you feel lost in the maze of cyberspace, technological advances, and the world moving ahead faster than you are?

Do you live with feelings of inadequacy, guilt, or fear?

Do you sometimes long for a spiritual center that can be a foundation for all you do?

If you answered yes to any of the questions on the previous page, you are in good company. An increasing number of people are becoming disenchanted with the tools our culture promotes as sources of "salvation." We are discovering the limits of technology, education, government, and careers. They do not provide ultimate happiness, peace, or contentment. As people become disillusioned with these traditional sources, they are beginning to look elsewhere. New Age, Eastern mysticism, and other faith patterns are claiming a place in our consciousness.

In the midst of this new world. a two-thousand-year-old faith proclaims, "Here is the answer to your spiritual search." Christians announce to the world that Jesus provides an avenue to wholeness and well-being—the way to the God whose power, love, and compassion are immeasurable. They reflect these words from the Bible:

"The Head of Christ," by Warner Sallman/Warner Press

I pray that the God of our Lord Jesus Christ, . . . may give you a spirit of wisdom and revelation . . . so that, with the eyes of your heart enlightened, you may know

what is the hope to which he has called you,

what are the riches of his glorious inheritance . . . , and

what is the immeasurable greatness of his power.

(Ephesians 1:17–19)

## Why Should I Read
### GET ACQUAINTED WITH JESUS?

GET ACQUAINTED WITH JESUS will

- help you discover who Jesus was;
- help you make your own decisions about what Jesus means in your life;
- help you decide what Jesus means for your world;
- offer you the opportunity to reflect on your beliefs, opinions, and behavior;
- guide you on your spiritual journey as you make faith decisions.

# "Who do you say that I [Jesus] am?"

Each of the first five chapters in this book will guide you through a segment of Jesus' life and ministry. You will explore his birth and childhood. You will walk with him as he travels through the region of the Middle East known as Galilee. You will explore his teachings and his storytelling style, and you will follow him through the last days of his life on earth.

The final two chapters will move you in a different direction. First, you will discover what early Christians said about Jesus as they struggled to tell the world about their new faith. Then, you will have the opportunity to examine what Jesus means to you.

This introductory chapter will help you get started. Here, you will consider what you believe about Jesus right now and receive some help in finding the places in the Bible where the stories and reflections about Jesus are found.

## Who Do You Say That I Am?

Jesus was surrounded by friends and followers who observed his activities, listened to his teaching, and witnessed his life. All this time, they were forming opinions about who he was. At one point, Jesus stopped and asked them, "Who do people say that I am?" They gave him a variety of answers. Then he asked, "Now, who do you say that I am?"

• How would you answer Jesus' question?

Use information you have heard from other people, or use your own life experiences. There are no right or wrong answers; this is only a first step. As you finish reading this book, you will be asked to return to your answer to see how or if your opinions have changed.

• Which of the pictures of Jesus in this chapter is most appealing to you? How does it represent what Jesus means to you at this moment in your life?

① Father, Friend
② Head of Christ.
   Approachable, soft,
   loving.

"Christ at Heart's Door," by Warner Sallman/Warner Press

## Going to the Source

The spirituality sections of libraries and bookstores are filled with books about ways to approach whatever is holy. Hundreds of books have been written over the centuries about Jesus, and even more speeches have been made. People have talked about Jesus, argued about Jesus, and formed opinions about Jesus.

Instead of talking "about" or reading "about," we need to go to the source. Reading the stories of Jesus directly from the Bible will help you more than any literature or conversation "about." We also need to interact "with" the Scriptures. The Bible is intended for two-way conversation. It gives you the opportunity to respond in ways that are appropriate for you—to ask questions, to listen for answers, to test new waters, to grow through the dialogue.

For this reason, this book will offer a "hands-on" experience. You will read directly from the Bible, and you will have the opportunity to "talk back" to the biblical authors. Through this process, you will find freedom to form your own opinions and beliefs.

You do not have to "know" anything ahead of time in order to walk through this material. This may be the first time you have ever worked with a Bible or seriously studied Jesus' life. That's OK! Do not be afraid to explore or even to make mistakes. We will give you the resources you need, and this introductory chapter will help you find your way through the Bible.

## How Do I Find a Bible to Use?

Bibles are not all the same! Some Bibles are translations, where a group of editors made a serious effort to convert the words of the original Hebrew and Greek authors into comprehensible English (or Spanish, or . . .). A few Bibles are paraphrases, where a writer interpreted the original authors in an effort to bring meaning to a contemporary world. We recommend using a translation. They can be found in many bookstores and, especially, in religious bookstores. The New Revised Standard Version of the Bible will be used in GET ACQUAINTED WITH JESUS. Other good translations include
* *Good News Bible*
* New International Version
* *Contemporary English Version*

"Christ Healing the Blind." Romanesque Fresco. Scala/Art Resource, NY

## How Do I Use the Bible?

The Bible is a book of books, sixty-six in all. It is divided into two major sections—the Old Testament (often called the Hebrew Scriptures) and the New Testament.

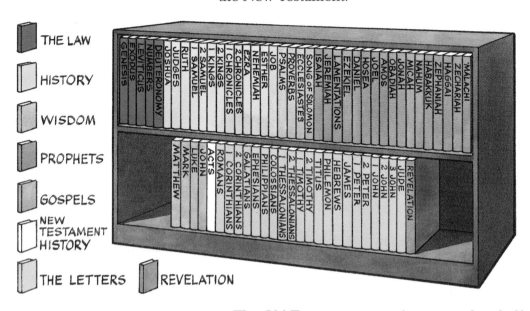

THE LAW

HISTORY

WISDOM

PROPHETS

GOSPELS

NEW TESTAMENT HISTORY

THE LETTERS    REVELATION

The Old Testament comprises more than half of the Bible. Its books include stories, poetry, history, and much more. The New Testament is the second major section of the Bible. In the New Testament, you will find the story of Jesus' life, a history of the life of early Christians, and letters/documents describing Christian belief and behavior.

Some Bibles number the pages in the Old Testament beginning with page 1 and continue through the end of the first section. Then, they begin with page 1 again as they move into the New Testament. Other Bibles begin numbering at the beginning of the Bible and continue to the end.

To help you find your way, the Bible is divided into chapters and verses. When you are studying the Bible, you will often be asked to look up a particular phrase, such as John 3:16. The word, in this case *John*, refers to the book title. You can find it in the table of contents.

The first number, *3* in this example, tells you in what chapter the phrase is found. Then, the chapters are divided into verses, which are sentences or phrases. The number *16*, used here, points you to the particular verse. (Sometimes, you will see a reference such as John 3:1-16. This simply asks you to read a series of verses within a chapter.)

Using your Bible, find the Book of John. (This is "John," not 1, 2, or 3 John.) Flip through the pages. Where do you find the chapter numbers? Find John 3. Do you see both the chapter number and the numbering of the verses? Now look up John 3:16. Does it say something like this?

"For God so loved the world that he gave his only Son, so that everyone who believes in him may not perish but may have eternal life."

## Bible Scavenger Hunt

This exercise is designed to acquaint you with the process of using the Bible and finding your way through the New Testament.

Look up the following. Match the references on the left with the word or phrase on the right.

| | |
|---|---|
| John 1:1 | Love |
| Matthew 5:14 | Bread |
| Mark 2:22 | All things new |
| Mark 15:14 | Wind |
| Luke 1:46-55 | Dawn |
| Luke 24:1 | Light |
| John 6:51 | Word |
| Acts 2:1-4 | Mary |
| 1 Corinthians 13 | Crucify |
| Revelation 21:5 | Wine |

## Some Final Questions

What attracted you to this exploration of Jesus' life?

What have you always wanted to know about Jesus?

What do you expect to gain from this book?

### Where Can I Find?

• The stories of Jesus' life?
  In the first four books of the New Testament. They are called "Gospels" and include Matthew, Mark, Luke, and John.

• Stories about the early Christians?
  In the Book of Acts, the fifth book in the New Testament.

• Letters and other writings about Jesus?
  Throughout the rest of the New Testament. Many were written by Paul; but others were composed by various authors.

## Prayer

Who are you, Jesus?
Some say you are ancient history;
Others claim you are the center point
For all of life.
Some say you are an icon in musty buildings;
Others find you in the heart-wrenching struggle.
Some are bored by you;
Others are invigorated by you.

Who are you, Jesus?
What is your claim on my life?

Whoever you are,
I come now
To seek,
To search,
To discover.

Questioning,
Hoping,
Wondering,
Tentatively trusting:
I am here.

Who are you, Jesus?

# CHAPTER 1

# BEGINNINGS

"Nativity," by Federico Barocci. Scala/Art Resource, NY

*In this chapter, you will experience*

- the stories of Jesus' birth
- one of Jesus' childhood adventures
- key events that marked the beginning of Jesus' ministry

"Safe in His Mother's Arms," by Wang Hon-yi, China, from *The Bible Through Asian Eyes*, by Masao Takenaka and Ron O'Grady

## Beginning at the Beginning

Jesus' beginnings left telltale tracks—tracks that, when followed, lead to the doorstep of all he did as an adult. In the beginning, the Bible says, Jesus' birth was extraordinary. A child of God and a child of a woman, he was born in a stable miles from any relative. His birth announcement, sent to the greatest and lowliest alike, shouted: "Here is the One you have been waiting for!"

Years drifted by. Jesus grew as any child grows and learned the carpenter's trade from his father, Joseph. Around the time he was thirty years old, however, life took a new turn. He visited his cousin, John, and was baptized in the Jordan River. Then, Jesus retreated into the desert wilderness to sort out his future. With the tempting time behind him, he moved forward to begin a new, public life of teaching, healing, and announcing the birth of a new day.

Joy to the World

"Joy to the world, the Lord is come!
Let earth receive her King;
let every heart prepare him room,
and heaven and nature sing,
and heaven and nature sing,
and heaven, and heaven, and nature sing."

What does it mean to sing "Joy to the World"? Has our God really come into our world? What happened in those days when Herod was king, when an honorable Jewish man and a young Jewish woman risked everything for their baby, when angels sang songs and the world was turned upside-down?

"Madonna of the Bamboo," by Carlos Francisco, Philippines, from *The Bible Through Asian Eyes*, by Masao Takenaka and Ron O'Grady

## What Does the Bible Really Say?

Can the following information be found in the Bible? Answer yes or no. (Answers on page 14)

1. Three kings came to visit Jesus.
2. Joseph's hometown was Bethlehem.
3. Mary rode to Bethlehem on a donkey.
4. Many angel voices told the shepherds of Jesus' birth.
5. An angel told Joseph to take Mary to Bethlehem.
6. Jesus' cousin John was born a few months before he was.
7. There were sheep and donkeys in the place where Jesus was born.
8. Jesus was born on December 25.
9. The angels sang, "Glory to God in the highest."
10. Mary's first response to the angel's announcement was puzzlement.

## Some People

*Some people would say
It is all nonsense.
And it is.
There is no reasonable,
rational explanation
for Jesus' birth.
Arguments
have raged
for centuries,
trying to bring
the light of reason
into the Story.*

*They have failed.*

*It is best
to greet the Birth
with faith
more like
a child:*

*To be entranced
by the wonder,
to accept
the mystery,
and
to live
the joy.*

**Key Concepts**:

*Incarnation*—Literally, "in the flesh." Jesus lived "in the flesh" with God's daughters and sons, experiencing life in its richness and its tragedy and pointing the way to amazing grace.

*Emmanuel*—God is with us.

*Jesus*—His name comes from the same root as "Joshua" and means "God is salvation." Hebrew people attached great importance to names, and Jesus' name points directly to his message and his ministry.

*Wise Men and Shepherds*—No one knows who the wise men were or where they were from. What is known is that they represented the finest people of the Gentile (non-Jewish) world. The shepherds, on the other hand, were among the poorest of the poor. They had little standing in their society. These two groups, from the opposite sides of society's spectrum, were invited to witness the birth of Jesus and gave evidence that God's birth announcement was to all earth's people.

| Stories of Jesus' Beginnings | |
| --- | --- |
| Isaiah 9:1-7 and Isaiah 11 | Prophecies concerning the coming of a Messiah. Other predictions scattered throughout Isaiah's writings. |
| Matthew 1–2 | The story of Jesus' birth from Joseph's point of view. The story of the wise men. The flight to Egypt. The slaughter of children in Bethlehem. |
| Mark | Mark has no mention of Jesus' birth. |
| Luke 1–2 | Stories about John the Baptist's birth. The angel's announcement to Mary. Mary's visit to Elizabeth. The story of Jesus' birth in Bethlehem. The angels' visit to the shepherds. Jesus' dedication in the Temple in Jerusalem. Jesus as a twelve-year-old in the Temple. |
| John 1 | There is no mention of Jesus' birth in John. Jesus as the Word of God. |

**Where Can I Find?**

Using the chart above, can you find the following?

"He named him Jesus." _____

"He is named Wonderful Counselor, Mighty God, Everlasting Father, Prince of Peace." _____

"Master, now you are dismissing your servant in peace." _____

"The spirit of the LORD shall rest on him." _____

"Do not be afraid to take Mary as your wife." _____

"Mary said, 'Here am I, the servant of the Lord.' " _____

"In the beginning was the Word, and the Word was with God, and the Word was God." _____

"My soul magnifies the Lord." _____

"Blessed are you among women." _____

"The light shines in the darkness, and the darkness did not overcome it."
_____

"She gave birth to her firstborn son." _____

"An angel of the Lord stood before them." _____

"Christ Between His Parents," by Rembrandt. Metropolitan Museum of Art, N.Y.

## Jesus as a Boy

Information about Jesus' childhood is sketchy at best. His early life is only mentioned once, in the Gospel of Luke. Here is what is known about Jesus' childhood:

- He grew up in a small town called Nazareth that was so far out of the way it was never bothered by invading armies.
- His father, Joseph, was a carpenter; Jesus apparently learned the trade from him.
- He was reared to be a Jew.
- He had a cousin named John.
- Jesus was an oldest child who had siblings.

Do you remember when you were twelve years old? What was life like for you at that age? Did you take any trips with your family? What happened?

Have you ever been separated from someone you love? What happened? How did you feel?

When have you been taught by a child? What did you learn?

How is Mary's question typically that of a worried parent? When have you reacted in a similar way?

How is this the "punch line" of this story? What does it say about Jesus?

41 Now every year his parents went to Jerusalem for the festival of the Passover. 42 And when he was twelve years old, they went up as usual for the festival. 43 When the festival was ended and they started to return, the boy Jesus stayed behind in Jerusalem, but his parents did not know it. 44 Assuming that he was in the group of travelers, they went a day's journey. Then they started to look for him among their relatives and friends. 45 When they did not find him, they returned to Jerusalem to search for him. 46 After three days they found him in the temple, sitting among the teachers, listening to them and asking them questions. 47 And all who heard him were amazed at his understanding and his answers. 48 When his parents saw him they were astonished; and his mother said to him, "Child, why have you treated us like this? Look, your father and I have been searching for you in great anxiety." 49 He said to them, "Why were you searching for me? Did you not know that I must be in my Father's house?" 50 But they did not understand what he said to them. 51 Then he went down with them and came to Nazareth, and was obedient to them. His mother treasured all these things in her heart. (Luke 2:41-51)

## Jesus in the Wilderness (Matthew 4:1-11)

Shortly after his baptism, Jesus needed to make a decision: What shape would his public ministry take?

So Jesus retreated into the wilderness, where he spent more than a month in solitude. (Later, such retreats became a pattern for him. Even in the busiest moments of his life, Jesus frequently went off by himself for periods of solitude, prayer, and contemplation.) While he was alone, the Bible says, Jesus was tempted to try three different approaches:

1. To be miraculous (Turn these stones into bread!);

2. To be spectacular (Jump from the roof of the Temple!);

3. To take authority and give in to the tempter (I will give you all the nations of the world if you will worship me.).

Jesus chose a fourth option: To worship God alone and to serve God unconditionally. When his decision was reached, the powers of temptation were gone and "angels came and waited on him."

## Jesus Begins His Ministry

If you were to write the purpose for your life's work in a single sentence, what would you say?

To be more specific, what do you hope to accomplish in your present career?

Without looking at the Bible, write below what you believe to be the primary purpose of Jesus' ministry.

Now read Luke 4:16-21.

Cleo Freelance Photo

"Saint Joseph and the Infant Christ," by Giovanni Battista Gaulli, called Baciccio. By permission of the Norton Simon Museum, Pasadena, California.

• How does Jesus' statement of purpose compare with your understanding of him?

• How does Jesus' statement compare with your life goals?

The Gospels of Matthew and Mark introduce Jesus' ministry in a slightly different way than Luke does. Instead of telling the story of his return to his home synagogue, they tell of his return from the wilderness to announce: "The time is fulfilled, and the kingdom of God has come near; repent, and believe in the good news" (Mark 1:15; compare with Matthew 4:17).

The word *repent* means literally "to change your mind" or "to turn around."

The phrase *kingdom of God* refers to a world where God's purposes are accomplished and all creation lives in peace.

Based on this information, which of the following statements do you think best describes what Jesus was saying:

• "I am God's Messiah! Change your ways! Believe in me!"

• "A new world is on the horizon. If you will change the course of your life and line it up with God's purposes, you will discover life as you have never experienced it before."

• "Turn from your wicked ways and follow the new course I will set for you, and you will discover what God's kingdom is really like."

---

## Answers

**1.** No. The Bible does not mention the number of people nor does it say they were kings. See Matthew 2. **2.** Yes. See Luke 2:3-4. **3.** No. There is no mention of how Mary got to Bethlehem. **4.** No. See Luke 2:10. **5.** No. The emperor's decree told Joseph to go to Bethlehem. See Luke 2:1. **6.** Yes. See Luke 1:26-37. **7.** No. The Bible does not mention any animals in the Christmas story. **8.** No. There is no solid information concerning the time of year of Jesus' birth. **9.** Yes. See Luke 2:13-14. **10.** Yes. See Luke 1:29.

Skjold Photographs

# Prayer

The angel said, "Hail!"
And Mary was
frightened.
The angel said, "Hail!"
And Mary said, "Surely
not I!"
The angel said, "Hail!"
And Mary whispered,
"Yes!"

The angel says, "Hail!"
And I too am timid.
The angel says, "Hail!"
And I answer, "Surely,
someone else!"
The angel says, "Hail!"
And I hear amazing
news.
The angel says, "Hail!"
God, give me courage to
whisper, "Yes!"

Amen.

# CHAPTER 2

# GALILEAN
# MINISTRY

Erich Lessing/Art Resource, NY

## In this chapter, you will encounter

- the location of Jesus' ministry
- Jesus' selection of his closest followers
- the miraculous events in Jesus' ministry
- women in Jesus' life
- an assignment given to seventy followers

## The Place

Jesus spent most of his public ministry in Galilee, located in the northern section of the country now called Israel. Galilee was diminutive in size, being only forty-five miles long from north to south and twenty-five miles wide. Its geography included rugged hill country, a large lake (sometimes called a "sea"), small villages, and fishing communities.

The population of Galilee was primarily Jewish. However, since a major trade route ran through it, a liberal dose of Roman citizens as well as people of other nationalities also lived in the region.

Jesus made his home in Capernaum (kuh-PUHR-nay-uhm), a city much larger than the hill town of Nazareth. Here he healed a Roman soldier's child as well as a man with "an unclean spirit." He participated in the life of the synagogue in Capernaum and often taught there.

Sea of Galilee looking toward Capernaum/Holmes Photography.

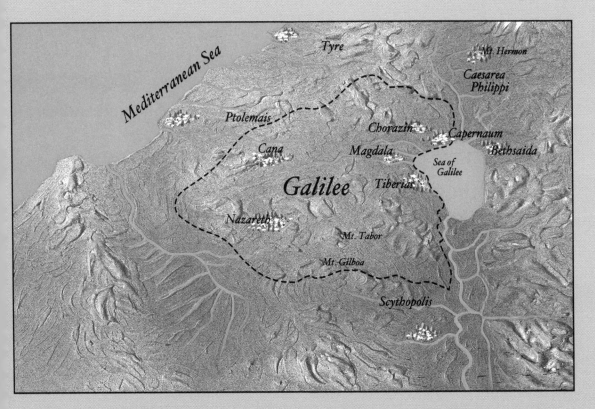

"The Calling of Saints Peter and Andrew," sixth-century mosaic from Ravenna, Italy. Scala/Art Resource, NY

## Call of the Disciples

Imagine it is a warm spring day. You are working outdoors, alongside your brother or sister, and life is good for you. A man approaches you. Perhaps you know him personally; maybe you know him only by reputation. He is a leader who is calling people to a new lifestyle of holistic health focused on radical obedience to God. He invites you to leave what you are doing and to follow him.

Will you

a. drop whatever you are doing and follow him?

b. tell him you have to have time to consider his offer?

c. turn down the invitation?

What is the reason for your choice?

Read Mark 1:16-20. How does your decision compare with the one made by these brothers?

## Focus Points

➜ A pool of water in Jerusalem was believed to have miraculous powers. It was said that whenever the water unaccountably stirred itself, the first person to enter the water would be healed. People suffering from disease crowded around this pool day after day, hoping beyond hope that they would be the one to enter the pool first and be healed.

One man had been waiting at the pool for thirty-eight years the day Jesus walked by. Jesus looked at the man and asked him, "Do you want to be made well?"

It was a profound question: Do you want to be whole? Examine the broken places of your life—the places of disease, the deep hurts, the alienation. Do you want to be made whole, or do you want to continue to live with the pain? The answer is not always as obvious as it seems.

For the rest of the story, read John 5:1-9.

➔ Jesus was teaching at his home in Capernaum that day, and a crowd had gathered. While he was teaching, some men brought a friend who was paralyzed to the house, hoping Jesus would heal him. Since the place was packed with people, they climbed up on the roof, carrying their friend with them. Opening a hole in the roof, they carefully lowered the man into the house until he lay in front of Jesus. Jesus looked at the paralyzed man and said to him, "Your sins are forgiven."

To *forgive* means literally "to let go" or "to release." What are the bonds or binds in your life that paralyze you? Where do you need to hear the words, "You are released; you are forgiven"?

For the rest of the story, read Mark 2:1-12

➔ Ten lepers begged Jesus for healing. Jesus sent them to the priests for an examination. On their way, their leprosy was cured. One man returned to Jesus and, shouting with joy, fell to the ground with gratitude. Jesus said, "Your faith has made you well."

Ten men were healed of their leprosy; one was made whole. The spiritual life plays a huge role in holistic health. How might your life be made complete through faith?

For the rest of the story, read Luke 17:11-19.

## Miracles

What would you call an event you experienced that you could not give a rational explanation for? Have you ever had such an experience? For the people who traveled with Jesus, such events were a way of life!

The Gospels (Matthew, Mark, Luke, and John) never use the word *miracle* to describe Jesus' activities. However, they do point to events beyond anyone's power to understand or explain. About thirty-five of these events are recorded. They include times when Jesus healed physical infirmities, when he "cast out demons," and when he exerted power over the forces of nature.

These miracles were never meant simply to display the spectacular. Instead, they focus attention on Jesus' authority even over the forces of destruction and evil. They say, in effect, "Here is your Messiah! Pay attention! Follow him!"

## A Sampling of Jesus' Miracles

Healing a Paralytic:
Matthew 9:2-8; Mark 2:1-12;
Luke 5:17-26

Calming a Storm:
Matthew 8:23-27; Mark 4:35-41;
Luke 8:22-25

Healing a Man With Demons:
Matthew 8:28-34; Mark 5:1-20;
Luke 8:26-39

Feeding Five Thousand:
Matthew 14:13-21; Mark 6:30-44; Luke 9:10-17; John 6:1-14

Walking on Water:
Matthew 14:22-33; Mark 6:45-52; John 6:16-21

Healing Ten Lepers:
Luke 17:11-19

## Calming the Storm

On that day, when evening had come, he said to them, "Let us go across to the other side." And leaving the crowd behind, they took him with them in the boat, just as he was. Other boats were with him. A great windstorm arose, and the waves beat into the boat, so that the boat was already being swamped. But he was in the stern, asleep on the cushion; and they woke him up and said to him, "Teacher, do you not care that we are perishing?" He woke up and rebuked the wind, and said to the sea, "Peace! Be still!" Then the wind ceased, and there was a dead calm. He said to them, "Why are you afraid? Have you still no faith?" And they were filled with great awe and said to one another, "Who then is this, that even the wind and the sea obey him?" (Mark 4:35-41)

Imagine you are with Jesus and the disciples in this boat in the middle of a raging storm. Looking at the picture, where do you see yourself?
- What are you doing?
- Is this where you have been in previous storms?
- How do you normally respond to a crisis in your life?
- How do you feel when the storm is over?
- What do you believe God is doing during the raging tempests of your life?

## Feeding Five Thousand People

The problem: five thousand people have gathered in front of you. They are hungry. You have no food to give them and no money to purchase supplies. Yet, it is your responsibility to see that all five thousand are fed. What are you going to do?

In the space below, list at least ten possible solutions to your problem.

Circle the options that have the best chance for success. Then select the best choice available to you.

Review Luke 9:10-17. How does your plan compare with the methods used by Jesus and the disciples? Record your thoughts in the space below.

What did you discover that might help when you want to respond to a human need in your community?

Biblical Archaeological Society

"Her Sins Are Forgiven," by Wu Yuen-kwei, China, from *The Bible Through Asian Eyes*, by Masao Takenaka and Ron O'Grady

## The Women in Jesus' Life

In the first-century world, men occupied the positions of power and authority in nearly every sector of life. The political arena was ruled by kings and emperors. Women were not even allowed on the main floor of the synagogue but listened from behind screened areas. Men held the position of ultimate authority in the home.

In spite of this, Jesus developed close relationships with both men and women and treated all of them as children of God. Men and women had access to his healing ministry and to his teaching. Women, as well as men, received him as a guest and a friend.

The women listed below all encountered Jesus in one way or another; each has a story to tell:

Mary, Jesus' mother: Luke 2:1-7; 8:19-21; John 19:25b (the second sentence in the verse)-27
Mary and Martha: Luke 10:38-42
Mary Magdalene: Luke 8:1-2; 24:1-12
Woman who was hemorrhaging: Luke 8:42b (the second sentence in the verse)-48
Woman who committed adultery: John 8:2-11
Peter's mother-in-law: Mark 1:29-31
Woman at the well: John 4:5-30
Woman who washed Jesus' feet: Luke 7:36-50

Select one of the women listed above. Read her story. Then, write her a letter:

Dear _____:

I just heard the story of your life with Jesus. My first reaction was:

Then I thought:

Some questions I want to ask you:

Because of you, I have learned that I:

In closing, I want to say:

Signed,

"Who Touched My Garment?"

**The Assignment**

Jesus once sent seventy of his followers into neighboring communities to carry out a specific assignment. Their story is found in Luke 10:1-12, 17-20.

What was the purpose of their assignment?

How many persons traveled in each group?

What were their instructions?

What resources did they take with them?

What were the results?

Based on this information, what "assignment" might be waiting for you?

What might be the instructions for you?

What resources would you need?

What will be the results?

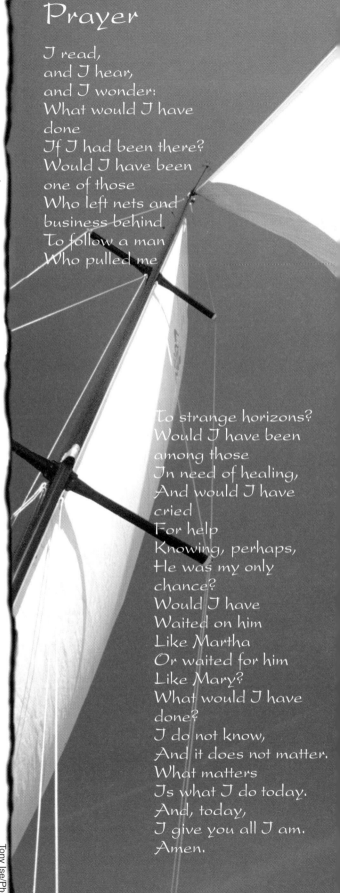

# Prayer

I read,
and I hear,
and I wonder:
What would I have
done
If I had been there?
Would I have been
one of those
Who left nets and
business behind
To follow a man
Who pulled me

To strange horizons?
Would I have been
among those
In need of healing,
And would I have
cried
For help
Knowing, perhaps,
He was my only
chance?
Would I have
Waited on him
Like Martha
Or waited for him
Like Mary?
What would I have
done?
I do not know,
And it does not matter.
What matters
Is what I do today.
And, today,
I give you all I am.
Amen.

# CHAPTER 3

# PASSION
# AND
# RESURRECTION

"Crucifixion," detail, by Xavier Jones/SuperStock

## In this chapter, you will experience

- the last days of Jesus' life, beginning with his Palm Sunday entry into Jerusalem and ending with the Resurrection

## A True Story: "I Don't Believe . . ."

The topic was "Resurrection." She was prepared to teach; her plan was in her hands and in her mind. The opening moments were concluded. The Bible passage and its meaning occupied her attention. Then, a class member spoke up.

"I don't believe that."

"What don't you believe?" she responded.

"I don't believe Jesus came to life again."

She took a deep breath and answered . . .

What would you say if you were the teacher of that class?

## Holy Week Timeline

**Entry into Jerusalem**
Matthew 21:1-11
Mark 11:1-11
Luke 19:28-40
John 12:12-19

**Several days of conversation and mounting tension**
Matthew 21–25
Mark 11–13
Luke 19:28–21:38
John 12:12–17:26

**Prayer in the Garden**
Matthew 26:36-46
Mark 14:32-42
Luke 22:39-46

**The Last Supper**
Matthew 26:17-30
Mark 14:12-25
Luke 22:7-30

**Arrest and Trial**
Matthew 26:47–27:31
Mark 14:43–15:20
Luke 22:47–23:25
John 18:1–19:16a

**Crucifixion and Burial**
Matthew 27:32-66
Mark 15:21-47
Luke 23:26-56
John 19:16b-42

**Resurrection**
Matthew 28
Mark 16
Luke 24
John 20–21

## Palm Sunday

Read Mark 11:1-11.

What does *Hosanna* mean?

*Hosanna* is a Hebrew word often translated "Praise God." Literally, it means "Please help" and is found in Psalm 118:25: "Save us ["Hosanna"], we beseech you, O LORD!" The word was sometimes used as a call for God's intervention in human affairs.

Why a donkey?

The image of a donkey appears in the Old Testament: "Your king comes to you; / triumphant and victorious is he, / humble and riding on a donkey" (Zechariah 9:9). When the Jewish people dreamed of their messiah, they imagined someone riding into Jerusalem on a donkey.

What's the point?

Any Jew would have immediately recognized what Jesus was doing. Fulfilling the words of the Old Testament, he was entering Jerusalem to inaugurate a new reign where God's kingdom would live on earth.

## Just Imagine

Just imagine you are one of the crowd on Palm Sunday. The hated Romans have tyrannized your world for over two hundred years. You cannot wait until the day comes when they will be obliterated from the earth. The rabbis have spoken for years of a messiah who will make things right. Now, Jesus—this teacher and healer from Galilee—is riding into the city on a donkey. Some people are shouting "Hosanna!" and waving branches in the air. What will you do?

Just imagine you are a Roman soldier assigned to guard the entrance to the city of Jerusalem. You hear a rabble-rouser named Jesus may be coming into town today. Along with other soldiers, you are constantly wiping out insurrections. Is this another in a long list? Jesus is now approaching. A mob is gathering. What will you do?

Just imagine you have followed Jesus for many months. You have listened to his teaching, observed his behavior, and followed his instructions. Recently, he told you death was waiting for him in Jerusalem. Now, as you prepare to enter the city, crowds gather. You hear the word *Hosanna*. What will you do?

## The Gathering Storm

Read Mark 11:15-19, 27-33; 12:13-27; 13:1-8.

Tensions ran high. Each day Jesus was in Jerusalem, the hostility grew more intense. One day he marched into the Temple, flew into a rage, and threw out the people exchanging money and making sales for the sacrificial offerings. The priests and scribes—meticulous caretakers of the law—were furious. Then a powerful religious group with government connections failed to trap Jesus in a question about resurrection. He told these people—who considered themselves biblical scholars—they did not know anything about the Scriptures or the power of God.

There were others. Those who hated giving any kind of allegiance to the government were offended when Jesus told them to "Give to the emperor the things that are the emperor's." Even the respected Pharisees were put off by his actions. Finally, Jesus even alienated the authorities when he predicted their magnificent buildings—the seat of power—would one day collapse. By the time of the Passover, Jesus was lucky to have even a few friends left. And even they were about to desert him.

## The Last Supper

"While they were eating, he took a loaf of bread, and after blessing it he broke it, gave it to them, and said, 'Take; this is my body.' Then he took a cup, and after giving thanks he gave it to them, and all of them drank from it. He said to them, 'This is my blood of the covenant, which is poured out for many' " (Mark 14:22-24).

## Gethsemane

Read Mark 14:32-42.

*I come with joy to meet my Lord,*
*forgiven, loved and free,*
*in awe and wonder to recall*
*his life laid down for me.*
*his life laid down for me.*

*I come with Christians far and*
*near*
*to find as all are fed,*
*the new community of love*
*in Christ's communion bread,*
*in Christ's communion bread.*

*As Christ breaks bread and bids*
*us share,*
*each proud division ends.*
*The love that made us makes us*
*one,*
*and strangers now are friends,*
*and strangers now are friends.*

What does this picture and its related Bible passage tell you

- about Jesus?

- about the relationship between Jesus and God?

- about yourself?

- about the way you make decisions?

## What Would You Do?

If you were one of Jesus' closest friends,
and if Jesus was in prison facing certain death,
and if his followers were likely to be arrested as well,
and if someone casually accused you of loyalty to Jesus,
What would you do?

What do you do now
when there is "something better" to do than worship?

when you are asked to accept a value system different from the way of Jesus?

To discover what Peter did, read Mark 14:66-72.

If you were a political ruler asked to execute a popular—and probably innocent—religious leader,
and if you could choose between making a decision and giving this "hot potato" to someone else,
What would you do?

What do you do now
when you are challenged by the human issues facing your community?

when a little voice whispers, "It's none of my business"?

To discover what Herod and Pilate did, read Luke 23:1-12.

### The Crowd Cried, "Crucify Him!"

The governor again said to them,
"Which of the two do you want me to release for you?"
"BARABBAS."
"Then what should I do with Jesus who is called the Messiah?"
"LET HIM BE CRUCIFIED!"
"Why, what evil has he done?"
"LET HIM BE CRUCIFIED!"
(from Matthew 27:21-23)

## Crucifixion

Read Mark 15:16-47.

To read the story of the Crucifixion, find a place where you can be by yourself. Move backward in time until you can be part of the scene. Perhaps you are an onlooker. Or one of the soldiers. Or Jesus' mother. Feel your way into the story. Let your emotions carry you through the last hours of Jesus' life.

Record your reflections about what you just read:

- an image:

- a feeling:

- a surprise:

- a question:

## Resurrection

Read Luke 24:1-12.

What would be your first reaction if you were the following persons? What would be your second reaction?

|  | First Reaction | Second Reaction |
|---|---|---|
| Mary Magdalene: | | |
| Two Men: | | |
| Disciples: | | |
| Peter: | | |
| Yourself: | | |

## Forced Comparisons

Forced comparisons can help you explore the mystery of the Resurrection. Choose one of the words listed below, and list six ways the choice you made is like resurrection:

**Mountain**       **Seashore**       **Phoenix**
**Puppy**            **Daylight**       **Rosebud**
**Prologue**        **Eagle**            **Garden**
**Night Light**     **Pine Cone**     **Dandelion**

**1.**

**2.**

**3.**

**4.**

**5.**

**6.**

Skjold Photographs

© M. Unselmann/H. Armstrong Roberts

H. Armstrong Roberts

Ron Benedict

## From Last Things to New Beginnings

Four women and men sat around a table during Sunday school at their small church. It was a somber gathering, for one of their close friends had just been told her son was dead. As they spoke, their class leader asked, "What helps you get through times like this?" One person answered,

"For me, the time of tragedy is like those last days of Jesus' life. When the crisis is anticipated, as in a prolonged illness or the break-up of a relationship, there is that Last Supper time of saying goodbye, of praying in the garden and wishing it could be another way.

"Then comes the time of death, sometimes physical, sometimes of a relationship. It is accompanied by shock, pain, and tears. Each person handles these moments in a different way.

"After the day of death comes Saturday. Someone described this day as a time of 'lying fallow.' The death is over; the healing is not yet. This is a critical time and cannot be hurried. Thoughts are gathered and lives are re-ordered. More tears are shed. We usually want this period to end quickly, but 'lying fallow' can sometimes take years.

"Eventually, the day of resurrection appears. Sometimes it approaches gradually, like a tiptoed presence in the dawn. You just wake up one day and realize you are alive again, that there is beauty around you and within you, and that life is glorious. You don't forget; you never forget. But you move on.

"Once you have experienced this cycle, you live in hope; for, when the next crisis appears, you know there will also be another resurrection."

## A True Story Continued: "I Don't Believe . . ."

She took a deep breath and answered, "Yesterday, I placed a piece of paper on a machine in my office. Thirty seconds later, the material on that paper appeared in another office 1,300 miles away. I don't begin to understand how that happened. I still wouldn't know even if you gave me all the details.

"But, you see, I don't have to know everything. I must realize some things happen that I don't understand. I have learned to be content with the mystery. And that is how I approach the Resurrection."

How does this teacher's response compare with what you would say?

## Prayer

Spend a few moments in deep silence. Sit very still with your spine erect. Take a few deep breaths. Let any energy or anxiety drain out of your body until you are totally focused. One by one, bring the following pictures into your inner "vision." Look at them carefully. Speak to them. Then let them slip away.

- Jesus rides into Jerusalem.

- Jesus breaks bread with his close friends.

- Jesus prays in the garden.

- Jesus dies on a cross.

- Jesus appears as resurrected Lord.

When you finish, remain silent for a moment. Be aware of any lingering thoughts, and speak with God about them. Then return to the living of your day.

# CHAPTER 4

# SERMON ON THE MOUNT

Modern chapel on Mount of Beatitudes, Israel/Three's Company

## In this chapter, you will

- focus attention on one of the most famous summaries of Jesus' teachings
- explore your own values in the light of Jesus' wisdom

## What Is the Sermon on the Mount?

The Sermon on the Mount is found in Matthew 5–7. (A sprinkling of the statements found in these chapters also appear in Luke, especially in the sixth and eleventh chapters.) It provides a powerful summary of Jesus' message. The truth contained in these three chapters transcends time. Here, Jesus speaks directly to the issues and challenges of our time: How can we live a balanced, spiritual life? How can we live in a healthy relationship with the people around us? In a world filled with "how-to" and "self-help" books, the Sermon reaches out and taps us on the shoulder. It challenges us to an alternative lifestyle.

## The Setting

According to Matthew, Jesus was sitting on a mountainside when his disciples gathered around him. This mountain has been identified as one just outside Capernaum and overlooking the Sea of Galilee. Given this backdrop, it is not hard to imagine the disciples sitting in a grassy meadow while Jesus offers his words of wisdom.

Read Matthew 5–7.

## What Can I Find in the Sermon on the Mount?

Jesus' teachings on
- The Beatitudes ("Blessed are . . .")
- Salt of the earth/light of the world
- Obeying the law
- Anger
- Adultery
- Divorce
- Retaliation
- Taking oaths
- Enemies
- Giving for others
- Prayer
- Fasting
- Wealth
- Worry
- The "Golden Rule"
- And more

## A Playbook for Life

Every summer, college and professional football teams gather across the United States to prepare for the fall season. After the players are selected, each one is given a large and complicated playbook to read and memorize. The playbook details the plays for both the offense and the defense. Once the players understand its content, they go onto the playing field to put their learning into practice.

In the beginning, they are disjointed and uncoordinated. Some are able to follow the rules; others have a hard time catching on. The day comes, however, when all the players are in tune with the playbook. Words are translated into action, and a team is born.

How is the Sermon on the Mount a playbook for life?

SuperStock

## "Blessed Are . . ."

The opening verses of Matthew 5 are called "The Beatitudes." They present a definition of the spiritual life that is very different from that promoted by our culture. At first glance, they seem absurd. At second glance, they appear to be impossible. At third glance, they just may deserve attention; for they point, not to weakness, but to strength.

Which of these Beatitudes is the most appealing to you?

Which one is the most challenging?

When do you feel you are most in tune with the Beatitudes?

What would it take for you to live your life with the Beatitudes as a foundation for your behavior?

# "Blessed are the poor in spirit."

Not: Blessed are those with poor self-esteem.
But: Blessed are those who recognize the ultimate poverty in their ability to create their own salvation and who know their need to depend on the God of life.

# "Blessed are those who mourn."

Blessed are those who are able to show emotion.
And also: Blessed are those who ache over the injustice that exists in the world.

# "Blessed are the meek."

Not: Blessed are the wimps.
But: Blessed are those who live humbly, who have a sense of who they are, who also value the people around them, and who realize that they are children of God.

# "Blessed are those who hunger and thirst for righteousness."

Blessed are those who are willing to sacrifice for the sake of justice and equity.

# "Blessed are the merciful."

Blessed are those who practice hospitality and who can stretch limits of compassion beyond their friends and families to include the outsider and the stranger in the street.

# "Blessed are the pure in heart."

Not: Blessed are those who live by the codes of deceit and violence.
But: Blessed are those whose lives are clearly focused, who are in tune with God, with their environment, and with one another.

# "Blessed are the peacemakers."

Blessed are those who believe there is an alternative to a violent world, who value nonviolent behavior, and who make peacemaking a verb.

# "Blessed are you when people revile you. . . ."

Blessed are you when people laugh at you and put you down when you stand up for what you believe.

Tony Ise/PhotoDisc

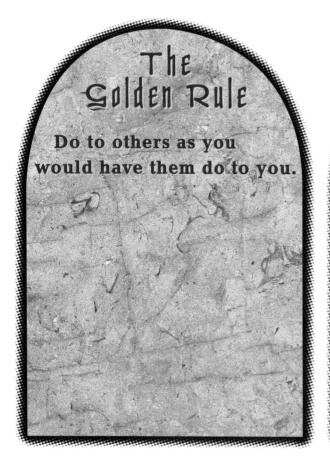

## The Golden Rule

**Do to others as you would have them do to you.**

## The Ten Commandments

1. You shall have no other gods before me.
2. You shall not make for yourself an idol. . . . You shall not bow down to them or worship them.
3. You shall not make wrongful use of the name of the LORD your God.
4. Remember the sabbath day, and keep it holy.
5. Honor your father and your mother.
6. You shall not murder.
7. You shall not commit adultery.
8. You shall not steal.
9. You shall not bear false witness against your neighbor.
10. You shall not covet your neighbor's house . . . or anything that belongs to your neighbor.

Which of the following statements do you prefer?

- If you live by the Golden Rule, you don't need the Ten Commandments.

- The Ten Commandments are God's law and must be obeyed.

### The Seven R's of Anger

The Seven R's of anger speak to the ways people respond to the anger within them. The first five are destructive. The last two offer possibilities for healing.

*The Destructive 5* →

Retribution: Getting what is coming to you. An eye for an eye, a tooth for a tooth.
Retaliation: Giving what's coming to him or her. Hitting back.
Remembering: Holding onto scraps from the past. Storing a treasure chest of hurts.
Rage: Anger out of control. Volcanic eruption of stored-up hurts.
Rippling: The infection of anger. Spreads like a virus out of control.

*Radical Reconciliation:*

Living in harmony instead of existing as adversaries.

Handling anger responsibly (Matthew 5:21-22).

Taking the first step toward reconciliation (Matthew 5:23-24).

Having courage enough not to escalate violence (Matthew 5:38-39).

## Forgiveness

Radical Reconciliation lives with a partner—forgiveness.

Anger is a heavy load to carry. It feels like a weight strapped to your back. The longer you carry anger with you, the heavier it gets. Forgiveness is, literally, letting go of the weight. To forgive is to say, "I do not have to carry this load any longer. I will not keep being loaded down by the weight of what someone else did. It is in the past. It is time to move on."

## Self-help

Choose the issue that is most critical in your life right now—Anger, Anxiety, Adultery, Divorce, Enemies, Fasting, Giving, Judging, Retaliation, Prayer, Profanity.

Imagine you are writing a self-help book telling people how to respond effectively to the issue you chose. In the space below, offer five "one-liners" summarizing the advice you will give.

1.

2.

3.

4.

5.

Browse through the Sermon on the Mount. Compare your response with what Jesus said. What are the similarities and differences?

Anger

Anxiety

Adultery

Divorce

Enemies

Fasting

Giving

Judging

Retaliation

Prayer

Profanity

> "Enter through the narrow gate; for the gate is wide and the road is easy that leads to destruction, and there are many who take it."
>
> Jesus

"*Ask, and it will be given you; search, and you will find; knock, and the door will be opened for you.*"

"Do not worry about tomorrow."

"Strive first for the kingdom of God . . . , and all these things will be given to you as well."

## "You are the light of the world."

"Do not store up for yourselves treasures on earth."

"Everyone then who hears these words of mine and acts on them will be like a wise man who built his house on rock."

How would you respond to the statements above if you were
- a new parent?
- struggling with cancer?
- planning for retirement?
- homeless?
- a "new" Christian?
- searching for a job?
- someone who has lived in the faith all your life?

How do you respond in your particular life situation?

## The Lord's Prayer

Read the Lord's Prayer below. [Note how the New Revised Standard Version's translation of Matthew 6:9-13 differs from the prayer you may be used to praying in worship services or your personal devotions.] What does each phrase mean to you? Write your response in the space provided.

Our Father in heaven,
   hallowed be your name.

Your kingdom come.

Your will be done,
   on earth as it is in heaven.

Give us this day our daily bread.

And forgive us our debts,
   as we also have forgiven our
debtors.

Jim Whitmer Photographs (All)

And do not bring us to the time of trial,
   but rescue us from the evil one.

Our Father . . .

**"Our Father in heaven, hallowed be your name."**

Augustine, in the early centuries of Christianity, said these opening words are already an answer to prayer, for the greatest thing we could ask is to approach the creator and ruler of the universe as parent or—in his word—father.

**"Your kingdom come. Your will be done, on earth as it is in heaven."**

God's kingdom is a way of life where all creation works in harmony with the will of the Creator. In reaching toward that Kingdom, we commit to a lifestyle where God's purposes come first.

**"Give us this day our daily bread."**

We do not ask to be consumers of the earth's resources. We ask simply for "the bread" we need. Perhaps we are also praying that all God's people will receive the bread they need as well.

**"And forgive us our debts, as we also have forgiven our debtors."**

We ask God to relieve us of the burden of any sin. *Sin* is defined in various ways in the New Testament—aiming for a target and missing the mark, deliberate disobedience, failing to measure up to expectations. Not only do we ask to have our burdens taken away, but we take the next step by "letting go" of any "sin" perpetrated against us by other persons.

**"And do not bring us to the time of trial, but rescue us from the evil one."**

In the ancient Jewish world, there was a belief that the end of the age would be preceded by a time of extreme testing, suffering, and persecution. This, then, became a prayer for rescue from persecution. We generally do not think in those terms, and our prayer is now one for deliverance from the sufferings caused by failure to obey the way of God.

**For yours is the Kingdom and the power and the glory forever.**

These words do not appear in Matthew but were used very early in the life of the Christian church. They are a closing affirmation that we ultimately live in God's time, not our time, that this is God's universe, not our universe, and that God is God for all eternity.

# Prayer

A breath prayer is a simple four-to-six-word conversation with God where you silently speak the first words as you inhale deeply and then speak the second words as you exhale slowly. It is meant to be repeated many times. Spend several minutes with the following breath prayer, or make up your own:

Fill me;
Use me.

# CHAPTER 5

# PARABLES

"The Return of the Prodigal Son," by Murille. National Gallery of Art, Washington, D.C./SuperStock

## In this chapter, you will

- experience Jesus as a storyteller
- encounter several of Jesus' stories
- explore the contemporary significance of Jesus' stories

## Some Background

What is a *parable*?

A parable is a story told to make a single point. Unlike an allegory, where every part of the story has a significant meaning, a parable is designed to carry the listener to a single truth about life.

Who told parables?

Storytelling was a common practice among the Hebrews. There is evidence in the Old Testament that adults used to answer children's questions with stories. When a child would ask, "What does this mean?" the keepers of the wisdom did not give direct answers. Instead, they said, "Let me tell you a story." The beauty of this kind of teaching was that the stories required the imagination and involvement of the listeners as well as the teachers.

Where can I find parables?

Jesus' parables are sprinkled throughout the Gospels. Matthew, Mark, and Luke include several of Jesus' parables in their recollections of Jesus' ministry. However, parables may also be found in the Old Testament. The Book of Job is a parable told to answer the question, Why do good people suffer? In 2 Samuel 12, the prophet Nathan confronts King David's adultery with a parable. The story was so ingenious David did not feel the full brunt of Nathan's condemnation until David—responding to the story—inadvertently judged himself.

## A Parable From the Writings of the Rabbis

For the Hebrew rabbis (teachers), storytelling was a common way of expanding upon the written words of Scripture. The following parable was developed as an explanation of a conversation Moses was supposed to have had with God. Moses asked God to: "Let everyone know what I have done wrong so that no one will say 'He falsified the books of Law' or 'He said something he was not commanded by God to say.' "

There once was a king who decreed, "Anyone who eats figs during the seventh year will be paraded in public so all will know the guilty one." It so happened that a woman was caught eating figs dur-

Ripe figs, Israel/Holmes Photography

ing the seventh year. As she was about to be put on public display, she pleaded with the King, "Please let everyone know the nature of my wrongdoing, so that people will not imagine I am an adulterer or a witch. For, if they see figs hanging from my neck, they will know what I have done and will not think even worse of me" (from a story found in *Early Rabbinic Writings*, by Hyam Maccoby; Cambridge University Press, 1988; page 177).

## The Prodigal and His Brother
Read Luke 15:11-32.

Who are the primary characters in this parable?


What role does each character play?


What do you believe to be the point of this story?

Jim Cummins/SuperStock

This parable and others were told as a response to criticism. Certain religious leaders accused Jesus of welcoming "sinners" and even eating with them. What do you believe Jesus was saying to these religious leaders?


What do you believe this parable says to you?


## The Oldest and the Youngest
Oldest children and youngest children in families are often quite different from one another. Oldest children are frequently the ones who take life seriously. They believe in the value of being responsible, on time, and in control. Duty comes before pleasure, and they often bear the weight of the world—for better or worse.

Youngest children, on the other hand, are frequently the charmers of the family. They are likely to be affectionate and even to appear to be carefree. Looking for attention, they can be the life in the family limelight—for better or worse.

Where are you among the siblings in your family? What is the role you play as the oldest, middle, youngest, or only child?

How did the two brothers in this parable behave as oldest and youngest children?

What can you learn from this story about the advantages and dangers of living out your place in your family structure?

## Feelings Chart

How might each of the characters in the parable of the prodigal and his brother have felt about the events that took place? List your ideas on the following chart. What do your replies tell you about your understanding of family relationships? of how God relates to you?

|  | Father | Oldest Son | Youngest Son |
|---|---|---|---|
| Youngest son asks for inheritance and leaves home. |  |  |  |
| Youngest son lives as a playboy. |  |  |  |
| Youngest son runs out of money and eats with pigs. |  |  |  |
| Youngest son returns home. |  |  |  |
| Father throws a party. |  |  |  |
| Father talks with oldest son. |  |  |  |

## The Good Samaritan
Read Luke 10:25-37.

The Setting:
   Who were the priests and Levites? They were leaders in the Temple charged with the responsibility of helping maintain the religious life. Priests performed the rituals and cared for the sacrifices, while Levites included teachers, musicians, and administrators. Both groups were meticulous in their understanding of and adherence to God's law.
   Who were the Samaritans? Hundreds of years before Jesus told this story, Israel was conquered by enemy forces. Most of the Hebrews were forced into exile. However, some people remained and mingled with the new culture being formed. The land in which they settled came to be known as Samaria. For a number of reasons, Samaritans were hated and avoided by Jews. To associate with a Samaritan was simply unheard of. Jesus shocked his listeners, therefore, by telling a story in which a Samaritan was a hero.
   What was this road? Jericho is an oasis village located near the Jordan River about seventeen miles east of Jerusalem. The road from Jerusalem to Jericho winds downhill among mountains in the Judean desert. It was an ideal highway for robbers, for they could hide behind one of the hills and wait for an unsuspecting and unprotected traveler to approach.

   Who might be considered a priest or Levite in your culture?


   Who might be a Samaritan?


   Where are your roads "from Jerusalem to Jericho"?


   What do you do when you travel these roads?

# What Would You Do?

What would you do in the following situations? Would you keep going, or would you offer to help? Why?

| | Keep going | Offer to help |
|---|---|---|
| 1.  You see a stranger with car trouble. | | |
| 2.  You are the first person to arrive at the scene of an accident. | | |
| 3.  You see a friend having trouble. | | |
| 4.  You see an older person having trouble with an ATM machine. | | |
| 5.  You are invited to work on a Habitat for Humanity project. | | |
| 6.  A homeless person asks you for money. | | |
| 7.  You see a child who appears to be lost. | | |
| 8.  You receive a telephone call from a charity asking for money. | | |

What does the parable of the good Samaritan say to each situation?

# When Have You Been?

When have you been like the thieves? When did you rob someone of their dignity? or of their well-being? or of their security? What was it like to be a "robber"?

When have you been like the man who was robbed? When has someone attacked you? hurt you? left you in pain? What was it like to be "robbed"?

When have you been like a priest or Levite? When did you go to the other side of the road to avoid involvement? What was your motivation? What was the result? What was it like to be a priest or Levite?

When have you been a Samaritan for someone? When did you help someone from no motivation except that they needed you? When did you care for someone different from you? What was it like to be a Samaritan?

When have you been an innkeeper? When have you been hospitable or caring because it was your responsibility to do so? When have you, just by doing your job, done something good for someone else? What was it like to be an innkeeper?

### The Lost Coin/Lost Sheep
Read Luke 15:1-10.

What's the point? What did these two parables mean

● to Jesus?

● to the people who first heard them?

What do they say to you?

"The Lost Coin," by Saw Edward, Burma, from *The Bible Through Asian Eyes*, by Masao Takenaka and Ron O'Grady

## The Bond

The bond was missing. I had taken it out of the safe deposit box only a few days earlier. When I went to cash it, I couldn't find it. Five hundred dollars had disappeared into thin air.

In the space below, list the things you would do to try to recover the missing savings bond.

Months went by. The bond was still lost. Even though I almost gave up, I kept looking. Perhaps it is in the file cabinet; or maybe in this pile of papers; or . . .

One afternoon, I was sorting through a stack of receipts I was saving for my income taxes. I first saw it halfway down through the pile. At first, I didn't believe it. But there it was. I had found the missing bond.

What comparisons can you make between this story and God's relationship with human beings?

What comparisons can you make between this story and God's relationship with you?

## The Sower

"Listen! A sower went out to sow. And as he sowed, some seed fell on the path, and the birds came and ate it up. Other seed fell on rocky ground, where it did not have much soil, and it sprang up quickly, since it had no depth of soil. And when the sun rose, it was scorched; and since it had no root, it withered away. Other seed fell among thorns, and the thorns grew up and choked it, and it yielded no grain. Other seed fell into good soil and brought forth grain, growing up and increasing and yielding thirty and sixty and a hundredfold" (Mark 4:3-8).

Think of a place in your life where you are playing the role of a sower. Perhaps you are unemployed and are looking for a job. Perhaps you are working on an experimental project. Perhaps you are parenting a child.

Biblical Archaeological Society

Read this story through the eyes of the challenge you just identified.

Circle the spot in the story that best describes your feelings about the growth of the "seed" you are planting. Why did you make this choice?

What else is this parable saying to you?

Imagine now that God is the sower and the seed is being planted in the field of your life. What kind of seed is God trying to plant in you?

Draw a square at the spot in the story that best describes how you feel about the current growth of God's seed in you. Why did you make this choice?

When are you most like a hard-packed path? rocky ground? thorns? fertile soil?

What does this parable say to you?

## The Day Laborers

If you were an employer and hired someone to work a full day, someone else to work a half day, and a third person to work a couple of hours, what salary arrangements would you make with each worker?

If you were hired to work a full day, how would you expect your compensation to compare with that of someone hired to work fewer hours?

Read Matthew 20:1-16.
Where do you see fairness in this story?

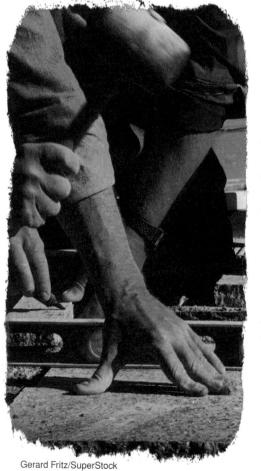

Gerard Fritz/SuperStock

Where do you see unfairness?

What do you believe is the point of this story?

In the space below, rewrite this story using one of the following to build your plot:

• You live in a nation where property lines are being redistributed. Much of your land is being confiscated and given to people you have grown to hate.

• Your father recently died, and his estate is being divided between you and his second wife's children. When the will is read, you discover he chose to distribute his assets equally among all of you.

• Eighty percent of the world's resources are consumed by people in the United States. You are part of an international task force to determine how to provide a better lifestyle for the earth's population who live in poverty.

• As a child, you are promised a trip to your favorite restaurant if you clean your room. You complete your responsibility only to find that your brother, who has done nothing, is coming with you.

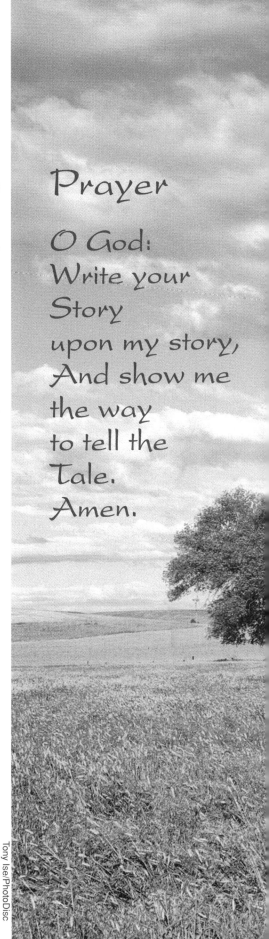

Prayer

O God:
Write your
Story
upon my story,
And show me
the way
to tell the
Tale.
Amen.

# CHAPTER 6

# EARLY
## BELIEFS
## ABOUT
# JESUS

Windows in a cavern near Antakya, Turkey, associated with the meeting place of the earliest group to be called "Christians"/Biblical Archaeological Society

## In this chapter, you will discover

- how the early church looked into the prophecies and discovered predictions of Jesus' life
- what two early leaders, Paul and Peter, said about Jesus
- how a statement of faith we call "The Apostles' Creed" summarizes what the church believes about Jesus
- what some early Christian leaders said about Jesus in letters, writings, and imagery

## Warm-up

Recall a powerful event in your life. Perhaps it was a moment of birth, or a tragedy, or a surprise. In the space below, describe that event and the ways it changed your life.

How accurate is your memory of this event? How would you find out? Is your interpretation shared by others who experienced this same event?

The followers of Jesus experienced a cataclysmic, life-changing event. They witnessed his teaching, his healing, and his ways with many different people. Then they walked through the days of crucifixion and resurrection. Afterward, they were left with the challenge of trying to explain what happened. Their efforts were not so different from what you experienced as you recalled something important from your life.

This chapter will explore several different efforts to describe what Jesus meant to individuals and also to the faith community called the church as these people began to reflect on their experiences and beliefs.

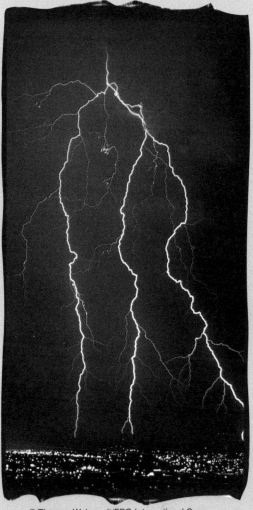

© Thomas Weiwandt/FPG International Corp.

## From the Prophets

As people tried to make sense out of their experience of Jesus, they looked back into their own faith traditions. They looked to the songs of their faith, which we call *psalms*. They also rediscovered the writings of men called *prophets*. These prophets were people of God who wrote of things to come. As these early Christians read the psalms and prophets, they began to see old words with new eyes. They said to one another, "These men must have been talking about Jesus!"

Listed at the top of page 56 are some quotations from the Old Testament that have been used to describe Jesus. Which ones do you believe were most important to early Christian believers? Which ones are the most important to you?

- "The Lord himself will give you a sign. Look, the young woman is with child and shall bear a son, and shall name him Immanuel" (Isaiah 7:14).

- "A child has been born for us, / a son given to us; / authority rests upon his shoulders; / and he is named / Wonderful Counselor, Mighty God, / Everlasting Father, Prince of Peace" (Isaiah 9:6).

- "The Spirit of the Lord shall rest on him, / the spirit of wisdom and understanding, / the spirit of counsel and might, / the spirit of knowledge and the fear of the Lord" (Isaiah 11:2).

- "He was wounded for our transgressions, / crushed for our iniquities; / upon him was the punishment that made us whole, / and by his bruises we are healed" (Isaiah 53:5).

- "Your king comes to you; / triumphant and victorious is he, / humble and riding on a donkey" (Zechariah 9:9).

- "I keep the Lord always before me; / because he is at my right hand, I shall not be moved. / Therefore my heart is glad, and my soul rejoices; / my body also rests secure" (Psalm 16:8-9).

- "The stone that the builders rejected / has become the chief cornerstone. / This is the Lord's doing; / it is marvelous in our eyes" (Psalm 118:22-23).

### Peter—A Background Check

If you can imagine a good-hearted man who often acted without thinking, sometimes made a fool of himself, and had a frequent case of foot-in-mouth disease, then you have a fairly accurate description of Peter. Peter was brash, impulsive, outspoken, and, perhaps, the most colorful of all Jesus' followers.

Peter was the one who

- immediately left his fishing nets to follow Jesus;

- stepped out of a boat to walk on water with Jesus—and nearly drowned;

- was one of the first to identify Jesus as the Messiah—God's Promised One;

- tried to convince Jesus to avoid Jerusalem and the cross;

- denied Jesus three times and then wept bitterly;

- ran directly into the empty tomb on the day of resurrection after the women brought him news of the empty grave.

It was also Peter who was bold enough and brave enough to be among the first to tell the world what he experienced. His is the first speech to be recorded in the Book of Acts.

## Peter's Speech

The Book of Acts tells the stories of the heroes who spread the good news in the years immediately following Jesus' death. An experience fifty days after the Resurrection sets the stage for the rest of the book. We call it *Pentecost*. Immediately after this experience, Peter stood up and gave an impassioned speech.

Read the story of Pentecost and Peter's speech in Acts 2.

List three statements Peter made about Jesus:

1.

2.

3.

What do you think was so powerful about Peter's speech that three thousand people changed their lives?

What convinces people to follow Jesus today?

## Paul—A Background Check

His name was Saul, at first. He was a leader in the Jewish community and a fanatic in his faith. Saul was therefore appalled when he discovered a new sect was undermining the beliefs of his tradition. He conducted a personal crusade to arrest and sometimes have executed any followers of this new "way."

One day, as Saul traveled to yet another city to oversee yet another round of arrests, he experienced the presence of the risen Christ. (Read Acts 9.) Then his life turned around one hundred eighty degrees. Saul became as committed to the way of Christ as he once was to the ways of his tradition. Eventually, Saul's name changed to Paul. He traveled extensively in the region of the Mediterranean Sea, telling the story of Jesus and establishing communities of faith. Paul was a prolific writer; some of his letters are now found in the part of the Bible we call the New Testament. (Read, for example, Romans, First and Second Corinthians, Galatians, and First and Second Thessalonians.)

Paul died, probably by execution, around A.D. 65 after spending several years in a Roman prison. To the end, he maintained his strong belief. In a closing letter to a friend, Paul said, "I have fought the good fight, I have finished the race, I have kept the faith. From now on there is reserved for me the crown of righteousness, which the Lord, . . . will give me on that day" (2 Timothy 4:7-8).

## What Paul Said About Jesus

Paul's Letter to the Romans summarizes his beliefs about Jesus. Read Romans 5:1-11 and Romans 8. Key statements from each passage are listed below. Read them again, and describe their meaning in your own words.

## From Romans 5:1-11:

## "Since we are justified by faith . . ."

## "We have peace with God through our Lord Jesus Christ . . ."

"The Flight of St. Paul from Damascus," Polish School. The Granger Collection, New York

"Christ died for the ungodly."

"We were reconciled to God through the death of his Son . . ."

## From Romans 8:

"There is . . . no condemnation for those who are in Christ Jesus."

"He who raised Christ from the dead will give life to your mortal bodies also . . ."

"All who are led by the Spirit of God are children of God."

"In hope we were saved."

"If God is for us, who is against us?"

"We are more than conquerors through him who loved us."

Review the statements above. Circle the one statement that is most important to you. Underline the one statement that is most challenging to you. Memorize the statement you wish to carry with you.

• Revelation 5:6—Lamb

• Revelation 14:14—Son of
Man seated on a cloud

• Revelation 19:11-16—White
horse and rider

## The Last Book

The last book of the Bible is an unusual book called *Revelation*. Written during a time of severe persecution to encourage Christ's followers to remain faithful at all costs, it is filled with word pictures and imagery. (You may wish to browse through the Book of Revelation to glimpse the range, flavor, and mystery of this unusual writing.)

Some of the images in the Book of Revelation describe Jesus. Examine the pictures on this page, along with their related Scripture references. Which of these images of Jesus is the most comfortable for you? Which is the most foreign? Which is the most surprising?

Now, create an image of Jesus of your own in the space below. You may want to choose an image from a favorite Bible verse or a hymn.

• Revelation 21:6—Alpha and
Omega

## Two Quotes and a Story

"[God] sent [Jesus] out of kindness and gentleness, like a king sending his son who is himself a king. He sent him as God; he sent him as man to men. He willed to save man by persuasion, not by compulsion, for compulsion is not God's way of working."

—From "The Epistle to Diognetus," A.D. 130–180. In *A History of Christianity*; Ray C. Petry, editor; Prentice-Hall, Inc., 1962; page 20.

MAKER OF THE SUN,
    HE IS MADE UNDER THE SUN.
IN THE FATHER HE REMAINS,
    FROM HIS MOTHER HE GOES FORTH.
CREATOR OF HEAVEN AND EARTH,
    HE WAS BORN ON EARTH UNDER HEAVEN.
UNSPEAKABLY WISE,
    HE IS WISELY SPEECHLESS.
FILLING THE WORLD,
    HE LIES IN A MANGER.
RULER OF THE STARS,
    HE NURSES AT HIS MOTHER'S BOSOM.
HE IS BOTH GREAT IN THE NATURE OF GOD,
    AND SMALL IN THE FORM OF A SERVANT.

—Augustine, A.D. 354–430. From *Leadership*; Vol. 8, No. 4.

In the year A.D. 155, or maybe 156, the aged Polycarp was dragged into the stadium to be thrown to the lions. One last time, he was questioned by the Roman proconsul:

Proconsul: Swear by the fortune of Caesar; repent, and say, "Away with the atheists."

POLYCARP: AWAY WITH THE ATHEISTS.

Swear, and I will set you free. Condemn Christ.

EIGHTY-SIX YEARS I HAVE SERVED HIM, AND HE NEVER DID ME ANY INJURY: HOW THEN CAN I SPEAK AGAINST MY KING AND MY SAVIOR?

I have wild beasts at my command. I will throw you to them unless you change your ways.

CALL THEM, FOR WE ARE NOT ACCUSTOMED TO REJECT WHAT IS GOOD IN ORDER TO ADOPT WHAT IS EVIL.

If you are not afraid of the beasts, I will burn you to death.

YOU THREATEN ME WITH A FIRE THAT BURNS FOR AN HOUR, BUT YOU ARE IGNORANT OF THE FIRE THAT BURNS TO ETERNITY. WHAT ARE YOU WAITING FOR? BRING ON WHATEVER YOU CHOOSE.

—From "The Sufferings of Polycarp," c. A.D. 155/156. Adapted from *A History of Christianity*; pages 44–45.

I believe in God the Father Almighty,

maker of heaven and earth.

And in Jesus Christ his only Son our Lord;
  who was conceived by the Holy Spirit,
    born of the Virgin Mary,
    suffered under Pontius Pilate,
    was crucified, dead, and buried;
  [he descended into hell;]
  the third day he rose from the dead;
  he ascended into heaven,
    and sitteth at the right hand of God the Father Almighty;
  from thence he shall come to judge the quick and the dead.

I believe in the Holy Spirit,
  the holy catholic church,
  the communion of saints,
  the forgiveness of sins,
  the resurrection of the body,
  and the life everlasting.
Amen.

## The Apostles' Creed

No statement of faith is more enduring in the Christian tradition than the Apostles' Creed. It is still recited in thousands of churches Sunday after Sunday. This creed was developed slowly, over hundreds of years. It may have begun in the early years as part of statements made at the time of baptism. It grew as early Christians responded to various "heresies" in the life of the church. Around the year A.D. 150 a statement of faith called the Roman Symbol began to circulate among the churches. It took a variety of faith statements and composed them into a single format. The Roman Symbol stated

I believe in God, the all-sovereign Father,
And in Jesus Christ, his Son:
The one born of Mary the virgin,
The one crucified under Pontius Pilate, and buried,
The third day risen from the dead,
Ascended into the heavens,
Seated at the right hand of the Father,
Whence he comes to judge the living and dead,
And in the Holy Spirit, resurrection of flesh.

The Roman Symbol continued to emerge over a period of several hundred years until, by the sixth century, it took the form now recognized as the Apostles' Creed.

Read the Apostles' Creed printed to the left. Choose one or two phrases about Jesus that are especially important to you. In the space below, describe the ways the statements you chose are important in your life.

How does the creed help you express your belief about Jesus? Try writing your own creed.

# Prayer

Christ, be with me,
Christ before me,
Christ behind me,

Christ in me, Christ
beneath me, Christ
above me,

Christ on my right,
Christ on my left,

Christ where I lie,
Christ where I sit,
Christ where I
arise,

Christ in the heart
of every one who
thinks of me,

Christ in every eye
that sees me,

Christ in every ear
that hears me.

Salvation is of
the Lord,

Salvation is of
the Christ,

May your
salvation, O Lord,
be ever with us.

—Saint Patrick, A.D. 389–461. From *The Communion of Saints*; Horton Davies, editor; Eerdmans Publishing Co., 1990; page 17.

Jim Whitmer Photographs

# CHAPTER 7

# WHAT DO YOU
# BELIEVE
# ABOUT
# JESUS?

SuperStock

## In this chapter, you will
- discover what other people say about Jesus
- learn ways Jesus has made a difference in people's lives
- decide what you believe about Jesus

## Getting Started

No one has stirred more conversation than Jesus. More volumes have been written about him, more speeches have been made about him, and more conversations have been engaged about him than any other human being in history. Still, people are asking, "What does it all mean?"

This chapter is designed to give some of the right answers. More important, it is designed to stimulate your thinking so that you will be able to say, "This is what *I* believe!"

## Sarah

Sarah was born on the island of St. Eustatius in the Caribbean in 1902. During her childhood years, she went to church on Sundays and Wednesdays. She went to church each Sunday having memorized one Bible verse and one hymn. She went to church on Wednesdays after memorizing yet another Bible verse.

So it was that, in her ninety-fourth year, Sarah lived with an accumulated memory bank of hymns and Bible verses. She could no longer sing on key, but the music was in her soul and on her lips.

One Monday morning, Sarah's back pain reached a crisis stage. The ambulance was called. She was transported to the hospital. Riding on the stretcher in the back of the ambulance, Sarah sang "How Great Thou Art" over and over again. She paused only when the ambulance hit a bump. Then she simply said, "Pothole," and returned to her music.

At the hospital, Sarah was soon diagnosed with terminal cancer. She returned home to spend her final days with family and friends. She died one week later. Two days before her death, she gathered her grandchildren together and sang to them:

"Jesus loves me, this I know,
for the Bible tells me so."

Sarah died peacefully—even joyfully—singing her way to eternity.

---

### He Comes to Us as One Unknown . . .

"He comes to us as One unknown, without a name, as of old, by the lake-side, He came to those men who knew Him not. He speaks to us the same word: 'Follow thou me!' and sets us to the tasks which He has to fulfill for our time. He commands. And to those who obey Him, whether they be wise or simple, He will reveal Himself in the toils, the conflicts, the sufferings, which they shall pass through in His fellowship, and, as an ineffable mystery, they shall learn in their own experience Who He is."

—From *The Quest of the Historical Jesus*, by Albert Schweitzer; A & C Black, Ltd., 1922; page 401.

## Songs Charles Wrote

Charles Wesley was a prolific songwriter during the eighteenth century. His music is still found in most hymnals.

Charles Wesley described Jesus in several different ways. Some of his images are reprinted in the chart below. In the space provided, write what you believe the phrase means. Then describe what you believe it means for you.

| IMAGE | WHAT THIS MEANS | WHAT THIS MEANS TO ME |
|---|---|---|
| Incarnate Deity | | |
| Hidden Source of Calm Repose | | |
| Sun of Righteousness | | |
| A Child and Yet a King | | |
| Love Divine | | |
| All Atoning Lamb | | |
| Lover of My Soul | | |
| Savior | | |
| Redeeming Lord | | |
| Sinner's Friend | | |
| Shepherd | | |
| Expected Guest | | |
| Judge | | |
| Joy of Heaven | | |
| The Name That Charms Our Fears | | |
| Hope of All the Earth | | |

## What Does Jesus Mean to You?

"In this modern, fast-paced time, Jesus brings forth a very simple meaning. Through Jesus' humanism, God was truly able to understand the feelings of love, despair, even death, and finally resurrection."—Bill, age 35

"For me, Jesus is a symbol of security and eternal love. Jesus is always by my side, smiling at me when I am in smiles and in tears."—Amanda, age 19

"God's unconditional love was given to all of us through his son Jesus Christ. He is our hope and provides continuous opportunities for love, grace, acceptance, and peace in the way we live our daily lives."—Debbie, age 39

"Jesus is the very 'standard' against which I try to gauge my life decisions and attitudes. When I fail to meet the standard, he is the one I turn to for consolation, forgiveness, and understanding."—Pat, age 24

"Jesus to me is an anchor in my times of distress. Jesus is a person who listens to me whenever I need him, a friend."—Marcia, age 34

"Jesus means God's teacher on earth. His lessons and teachings provide the answers to my human struggles, if I will only choose his way."—Laurie, age 42

Jim Whitmer Photographs

Jim Whitmer Photographs

Jim Whitmer Photographs

Skjold Photographs

# Lord
## of the
# Dance

I danced in the morning when the world was begun,
  and I danced in the moon and the stars and the sun,
and I came down from heaven and I danced on the earth.
  At Bethlehem I had my birth.

I danced for the scribe and the Pharisee,
  but they would not dance and they would not follow me;
I danced for the fishermen, for James and John;
  they came to me and the dance went on.

I danced on the sabbath when I cured the lame,
  the holy people said it was a shame;
they whipped and they stripped and they hung me high;
  and they left me there on a cross to die.

I danced on a Friday and the sky turned black;
  it's hard to dance with the devil on your back;
they buried my body and they thought I'd gone,
  but I am the dance and I still go on.

They cut me down and I leapt up high,
  I am the life that'll never, never die;
I'll live in you if you'll live in me;
  I am the Lord of the Dance, said he.

Refrain:
Dance, then, wherever you may be;
  I am the Lord of the Dance, said he.
And I'll lead you all wherever you may be,
  and I'll lead you all in the dance, said he.

—LORD OF THE DANCE, words: Sydney Carter. © 1963 by Stainer & Bell Ltd. Used by permission of Hope Publishing Co.,
Carol Stream, IL 60188. All rights reserved. Used by permission.
Ron Benedict

## I Am . . .

According to the Gospel of John, Jesus defined himself and his ministry with a series of "I Am" statements. These metaphors intended to describe Jesus' life and ministry in ways that would make sense to first-century Christians. As you read each of the "I Am" statements below, what pictures or images come to mind? Capture your thoughts with words or drawings in the "Doodle Space" below.

**"I am the bread of life. Whoever comes to me will never be hungry, and whoever believes in me will never be thirsty."**
—John 6:35

*"I am the light of the world. whoever follows me will never walk in darkness but will have the light of life."*—John 8:12

"I am the gate. Whoever enters by me will be saved, and will come in and go out and find pasture."—John 10:9

**"I am the good shepherd. The good shepherd lays down his life for the sheep."**—John 10:11

"I am the resurrection and the life. Those who believe in me, even though they die, will live, and everyone who lives and believes in me will never die."—John 11:25-26

"I am the way, and the truth, and the life. No one comes to the Father except through me."—John 14:6

"I am the true vine, and my Father is the vinegrower."
—John 15:1

## Pictures of Jesus

*Jesus throwing out the moneychangers*

To some people, Jesus was the activist calling for a radically different way of life. He identified with the poor, the disenfranchised, and the outcasts. He challenged the existing systems and structures, calling them to a higher purpose.

To these people, Jesus' message to contemporary society is found in the words, "Just as you did it to one of the least of these who are members of my family, you did it to me" (Matthew 25:40).

*Jesus knocking at the door*

To some people, Jesus is "Lord and Savior." He is the stable force in an uncertain world. Jesus died and rose again to invite all God's people to a life of saving grace. To those who come to him in faith he offers freedom from bonds and binds, a secure future, and a promise of eternity. He is summarized in the words of the song, "Amazing grace! How sweet the sound that saved a wretch like me! I once was lost, but now am found; was blind, but now I see."

To these people, Jesus' message to contemporary society is summarized in his words, "I am the way, and the truth, and the life."

Warner Press

*Laughing Jesus*

To some people, Jesus was an extraordinary human being—a friend and a lover of humanity. As a child, he laughed and cried and sometimes upset his parents. As an adult, he pointed to the One who walks alongside us in the joys and struggles of life. He showed us that God joins our parties and celebrations, just as Jesus once attended a wedding banquet. God also grieves with us in our sorrow and weeps as Jesus once did for a friend.

To these people, Jesus' message to contemporary society is found in two images: "There was a wedding in Cana. Jesus had been invited" (adapted from John 2:1-2) and "Jesus began to weep" (John 11:35).

Fellowship of Merry Christians

*Jesus healing a blind man*

To some people, Jesus was a healer. He brought health and wholeness to people who lived without hope. He brought wellness to both body and soul and was an advocate of holistic health. He pointed to God as the source of all healing and well-being. Persons who are dis-eased can go to God and find the prescription to bring them life.

To these people, Jesus' message to contemporary society is summarized in the phrase, "Your faith has made you well; go in peace" (Luke 8:48).

Scala/Art Resource, NY

*Sallman's head of Jesus*

To some people, Jesus offers peace and serenity. They find in Jesus a calm assurance. He is their rock, the foundation on which they can build the rest of their lives. Their security is in the knowledge that Jesus walks with them through each day of their lives. They have in Jesus a reliable source in which they place unqualified trust.

To these people, Jesus' message to contemporary society is summarized in the statement, "Come to me, all you that are weary and are carrying heavy burdens, and I will give you rest" (Matthew 11:28).

Which of the pictures on these pages comes closest to your image of Jesus?

Warner Press

Which picture is the most uncomfortable for you? Why?

Compare your feelings now with the response you made on page 4 as you began reading this book.

## Who Do You Say That I Am?

At the beginning of this book, you read about an encounter between Jesus and Peter. Jesus had been asking his friends what people were saying about him. After listening to their answers, he asked, "Who do you say that I am?" (Matthew 16:13-20).

Without looking back to your earlier comments, answer Jesus' question as if he were asking you personally:

● "Who do you say that I am?"

Now compare your comments with the way you answered the question earlier.

Where have your opinions changed as you became better acquainted with Jesus?

What beliefs remain the same?

What questions do you still have?

*Prayer*

*Dear God,*

*Because of my understanding of Jesus, I now believe you . . .*

*I also believe I am . . .*

*In the days and weeks ahead, please help me . . .*

*Now, I commit myself to . . .*

*Amen.*

y Ise/PhotoDisc